Knotting & Netting

Knotting & Netting

The Art of Filet Work

Lisa Melen

VAN NOSTRAND REINHOLD
NEW YORK   CINCINNATI   LONDON   TORONTO   MELBOURNE

This book was originally published in Swedish under the title *Knutet och Trätt* by I.C.A. Forlaget, Vasteras, Sweden *Knutet och Trätt* copyright © Lisa Melen and I.C.A. Forlaget 1971

Translated from Swedish by Joan Bulman English translation © Van Nostrand Reinhold Company Ltd., 1972

Photographs by Bertil Lindh.
Photographs on pages 8 and 12 reproduced courtesy of the National Museum Reykjavik and Nordiska Museum, Stockholm.
Library of Congress Catalog Card Number 72–1857
ISBN 0 442 29958 3

This book is set in Apollo and is printed in Great Britain by Jolly & Barber Ltd., Rugby and bound by the Ferndale Book Company.

Published by Van Nostrand Reinhold Company, Inc., 450 West 33rd St., New York N.Y. 10001 and Van Nostrand Reinhold Company 25–28 Buckingham Gate, London SW1E 6LQ.

Published simultaneously in Canada by Van Nostrand Reinhold Company Ltd.

Van Nostrand Reinhold Company Regional Offices: New York Cincinnati Chicago Millbrae Dallas.

Van Nostrand Reinhold Company International Offices: London Toronto Melbourne.

16 15 14 13 12 11 10 9 8 7 6 5 4 3 2 1

Contents

Preface

The ancient technique of netting and embroidering on net is now undergoing a revival, and this handbook has been prepared for all who wish to know more about it. Many beautiful old patterns have been preserved and they provide inspiration for new designs; at the same time, anyone can develop his or her own designs using the basic technique.

There are two main branches to this craft: using net with a diamond mesh and using net with a square mesh. Historical and contemporary examples of both techniques are shown in this book.

The skill is easily learnt; the tools required are few and simple; and many people find it completely absorbing.

Lisa Melen

Count Claes Julius Ekeblad netting while his wife reads aloud. Painting by Lars Sparrgren of the manor house, Stola, Västergötland, in 1783 (Nordiska Museum, Stockholm).

History

If we want to trace the history of netting we shall have to go as far back as the Egyptian burial chambers, where net has been found richly embroidered with pearls and precious stones.

In Greek mythology Aphrodite rose every morning out of the sea and gathered round her women whom she taught to make net, to spin with the distaff and to weave.

In Norse mythology it was Loki who discovered the art of netting. He was pursued by the gods and took refuge in a lake, where he supported himself by catching fish in a net he had made with his own hands. The gods captured him and then he had to teach them the art of netting.

During the Middle Ages netting was used for church textiles and magnificent articles were made in gold and silver, linen and silk. The net itself was made of silver or gold thread, and the patterns were embroidered in linen and silk by nuns. The figures used for the patterns were usually taken from the Bible, such as angels and apostles and animal figures from the Book of Revelations.

In the seventeenth century, when the art of netting reached its peak, linen yarn began to be used for darning the net. Other stitches used at this time to enrich the embroidery included satin stitch, chain stitch, shaded stitch, buttonhole stitch and woven wheels, all under the general name of *filet guipure*. There was a great vogue at the time for anything foreign, which was why the French name was retained. The rich ornamentation of *filet guipure* calls for larger mesh and coarser yarn than is used nowadays for net embroidery.

During the eighteenth and nineteenth centuries netting was done all over Scandinavia, including Iceland. The net was used for roof hangings, both in the houses of the gentry and in the humblest cottages. The textile art of the peasantry was strongly influenced by that of the upper classes, who often obtained their magnificent textiles from Italy and France. Festive panels and hangings were also made of net to adorn the great rooms on special occasions. There are many such pieces of embroidery preserved in Scandinavian museums (see illustrations on pp. 11–17).

In the nineteenth century both square and diamond mesh net was made all over Sweden. A special kind of embroidered net (*pinnspets*), using only two embroidery stitches – ordinary darning stitch and cross stitch – on a ground of diamond mesh, was practised particularly in northern Sweden. This local variant was found also in Värmland, Småland and northern Skåne, but in the rest of the country embroidery over square mesh was most common.

Following a period of neglect netting began to be popular again during the first decade of the twentieth century, when industrious fingers turned out the most fantastic work. Tablecloths, cushions, curtains, edgings for sheets, mittens and night-caps were netted and embroidered, all in the most complicated patterns. Round doilies were also very popular at this time, the variegated pattern being produced by using mesh sticks of different widths.

In England the French names *filet* and *lacis* are associated with this type of embroidery. During the Victorian era, when it was much in vogue, it was also known as *guipure d'art,* and the French names for the stitches were also used. By the end of the nineteenth century a commercially made net was normally used instead of a handmade one. However, a knowledge of the method of constructing the net, as well as of embroidering it, gives scope for imaginative and original work today.

Roof hanging from Rakeby parish in the county of Skaraborg, marked 1826. The hanging, which was used for adornment, has three inset panels of embroidered net. The net, which has meshes 1 cm ($\frac{3}{8}$ in) across, is made and embroidered with the same thread – a handspun, firmly twisted linen yarn. The pattern is worked in cloth stitch. The fabric in which the net is inserted is of plain weave and finished with a fringed edging 15 cm (6 in) wide made by knotting the warp of the base fabric after the weft threads have been withdrawn (Västergötland Museum, Skara).

Chalice cloth made of linen yarn from Iceland, 55 × 52 cm (21¾ × 20½ in). Circa 1700. The inscription is a verse of a psalm, translated from the Danish and including the letters I.O.D. and M.K.E.V. The first set of letters are presumably the initials of the woman who made the cloth and the second set, those of the church that owned it (Icelandic National Museum, Reykjavik).

Detail of lace in *filet guipure,* netted and embroidered in 1863 from a French original. Netting and embroidery are in white cotton yarn (in private ownership).

Lace edging, embroidered on net in firmly twisted cotton yarn from
a French original. Circa 1863 (in private ownership, photo on left).
Detail of a large cloth, 120 × 200 cm (48 × 80 in), made in 1875 in
Hudiksvall (in private ownership, photo below).

Mat in square mesh net. Made circa 1924. Diameter of mat 36 cm (14$\frac{3}{8}$ in) (in private ownership).

Mat in square mesh net, made in 1920 of firmly twisted cotton yarn.

Materials

Netting needle
Mesh sticks in various widths
Soft board (pin board) covered with 5 mm (or $\frac{1}{4}$ in) squared paper and transparent adhesive paper (Fablon or other transparent book-covering film)
Linen thread 35/3 (Holma Hälsingland) for netting
Linen yarn no. 16 half-bleached and unbleached, and lace thread 18/3 and 18/5 Holma Hälsingland's Linspinneri (flax mill). NIAB's allmogegarn (peasant or country yarn) colour 606 and 607 or 603 and 604. These yarns are used for embroidery. Other threads suitable for netting are crochet yarns and pearl cotton (*coton perlé*). *Coton à broder* and stranded cotton are suitable for the embroidery
Tapestry needles no. 18
Glass-headed pins
Frame
Rug warp 12/6 (linen thread or fine strong twine) to stretch the net
Pin cushion filled with sand or shot, or drawing pin to fix the stirrup to
In case of difficulty all the materials can be obtained from
Skaraborgs läns hemslöjdsförenings filial, Gamla Rådhuset,
531 01 Lidköping, Sweden.

Washing advice

Embroidered net must be washed with great care. Use soap-flakes and rinse thoroughly. Lay the work between two towels to remove most of the moisture; then stretch it out, wrong side up, either on the soft board or in a frame and paint it over with gelatine solution. The work will be dry in a couple of hours and can then be removed from the board or frame.

From the top downwards: mesh stick; netting needle; and needle
loaded with thread.

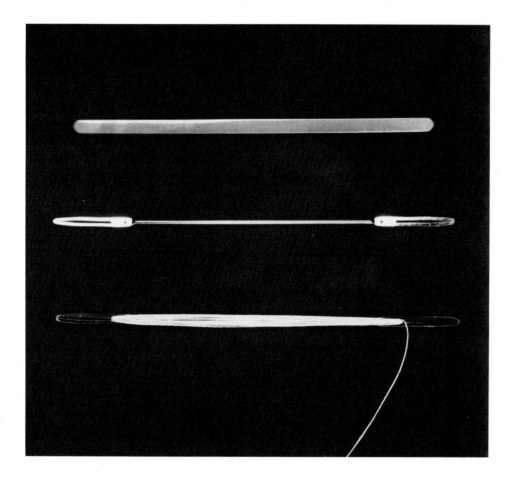

Making net

To make net you will need a netting *needle,* made of metal, horn or wood, with closed prongs at the end which are elastic enough to open and close easily. In metal needles there is usually a small hole in which the thread is fastened. Wind the thread on to the needle (see illustration p. 19). Do not load the needle too heavily, as then it will not slip easily through the meshes. A *mesh stick* is used to ensure that the meshes are all exactly the same size. This may be of metal, horn or wood and of various widths, but it must be smooth and even. Each stitch will be as large as the diameter of the mesh stick used. Make a large loop, called the foundation loop, and fix this over a pin stuck into a small but heavy pin-cushion. This may appropriately be filled with lead shot or sand to make it sufficiently heavy. The loop may also be attached to a drawing-pin or tin-tack, fixed under the edge of a table or some such place. The net may be made with any thread – linen, silk, cotton or metal thread or ordinary rug warp – provided that it is firmly twisted, strong and smooth. In Sweden the thread which is most popular and which has proved very suitable is Holma Hälsingland's linen thread 35/3.

Avoid untwisting the thread too much. If this should happen let the threaded needle hang downwards so that the thread can twist itself up again. Only embroider perfectly made net: uneven or badly knotted net can never do justice to the work.

The knot is always made the same way, whether for net with square or diamond mesh. Begin by making a loop, the 'foundation loop', of single thread. It is into this that the first stitch will be knotted. Hang the loop over one or more strong pins stuck into the cushion filled with sand or shot.

The thread to be used for netting is firmly knotted to the loop. Hold the mesh stick in your left hand, keeping your fingers straight. Lay the mesh stick between your thumb and first finger, close against the loop, and hold the needle in your right hand.

Bring the thread down in front of the mesh stick and round the third finger of your left hand, up behind the mesh stick and along your first finger, in front of the loop and over to your thumb, which holds the thread firmly down.

Bring the thread round in a wide loop towards your left shoulder, back again behind the mesh stick and down behind all the fingers of your left hand. Continuing round your little finger, insert the needle upwards through the loop on your third finger, underneath the mesh stick and into the foundation loop from below. A second loop is thus formed, held open by your little finger.

At the same time as the needle is inserted through the loops, your thumb releases its grip on the thread. The first loop round your third finger is slipped off, the second loop being retained by your little finger.

The needle thread is now drawn tight and the knot worked up to the upper edge of the mesh stick with the aid of the loop on your little finger. When it is firmly in place, slip the loop off your little finger and draw downwards. The knot will then be fast and firm.

Net with square meshes (Filet)

To make square-meshed net cast two stitches, as already described, on to the foundation loop, draw out the mesh stick and turn the work (netting is always worked from left to right). Increase by netting two stitches into the last loop of every row. To make a square cloth, when you have reached the necessary width work one row without increasing, then decrease by netting one stitch into two loops together at the end of each row. Tie the last two loops together.

To make a long strip in square mesh (e.g. a piece of lace) start with a foundation loop and cast two stitches on to it (see illustration p. 28). You start work from one corner, netting backwards and forwards and increasing one stitch at the end of each row by netting two stitches into the last loop. Continue until you have reached the desired width. Then start decreasing on one side, by netting one stitch into two loops together at the end of the row. The width will remain constant if you always increase one stitch at the end of the row on the other side. When the strip is long enough, decrease at the end of every row.

To make a piece of net with square meshes, start with a foundation loop on which you have cast two stitches.

Always work from left to right and increase by netting two stitches into the last stitch in each row.

To make an oblong piece of net, once you have reached the desired width decrease by netting the last two loops together on one side while continuing to increase on the other side.

When the strip is long enough, net the last two stitches together on both sides.

Net with diamond mesh

To make net with diamond mesh start by making a foundation loop and cast on stitches as described on pp. 21–26. You must cast as many stitches on to the foundation loop as you will need for the net you are making. (Note that it is always the stitches that lie *underneath* each other that you count.) When the first row of stitches is completed slip out the mesh stick and work another row of stitches into the loops left in the previous row. In making a large net it will be necessary to slip some of the stitches off the mesh stick from time to time.

When the net is completed pull out the foundation loop and unpick the cast-on knots that are on it. This means that the knots of the first row of meshes are set free and the meshes made larger than those of the succeeding rows. It is therefore a good idea to use a mesh stick for the first row 1 mm (fractionally) smaller than that used for the rest of the work.

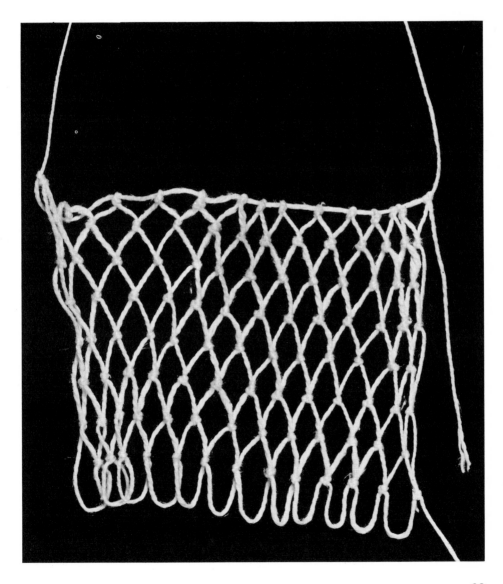

Round nets

To make a netted circle, start in the same way as for net with diamond mesh; i.e. cast the required number of stitches on to a foundation loop. When it comes to working the second row, pull up the stitches to close the circle, do not turn the work but knot the thread into the first stitch without forming a loop. Increase by working two knots into the loops of the previous row where required to keep the work flat. Work row after row, slipping out the mesh stick from time to time as it is difficult to work with too many stitches on it. Always leave 3–4 stitches on the mesh stick.

Patterns may be worked into round mats in a number of ways. You can net several stitches into one stitch in the previous row and then draw them together by netting several stitches together so as to form a hole. You can also decrease by netting into each alternate stitch. Different widths of mesh stick may also be used to produce a rich pattern.

Joining threads

Threads are joined by using a weaver's knot: hold one thread in your left hand, the other in your right. Hold the threads between your thumb and first finger. Lay the thread in your right hand behind the one in your left (illustration at the top of p. 37).

Bring the end of the thread in your right hand forward over and round your thumb, up behind the other end of the same thread and back in front of your left hand (illustration in the centre).

The left end is turned in under the loop round your thumb, which is released. Draw both ends of the right-hand thread tight towards the right while drawing both left-hand threads to the left. This forms a knot which is supple and strong (bottom illustration).

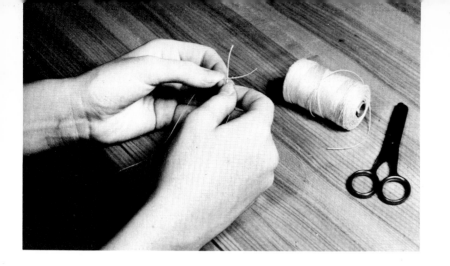

Stretching net

When the net is finished it is stiffened in a solution of three leaves of gelatine in a half coffee-cupful of water. Put the gelatine with the water in a bowl to dissolve. Put in the net and let it soak through, then lay it on a piece of kitchen paper to remove most of the moisture. If the net is small it will be easiest to stretch it on a pin-board covered with 5 mm ($\frac{1}{4}$ in) squared paper with transparent Fablon on top. It will then be easy to stretch the net out straight by sticking pins in the meshes (see pp. 39 and 40). Allow to dry. With a larger net it will be better to stretch it in a frame. It will be easier to do this before it is put in the gelatine solution. Thread a tapestry needle no. 18 with rug warp 12/6, or fine strong thread or twine, and run it from each mesh to the corresponding nail in the frame (see illustration p. 41). Stretch the net carefully and evenly and then paint it all over with gelatine solution, using a broad paintbrush. Allow the net to dry.

Square mesh net stretched on a pin-board covered with squared paper and a transparent adhesive paper such as Fablon. It can easily be kept straight by aligning it with the lines on the graph paper.

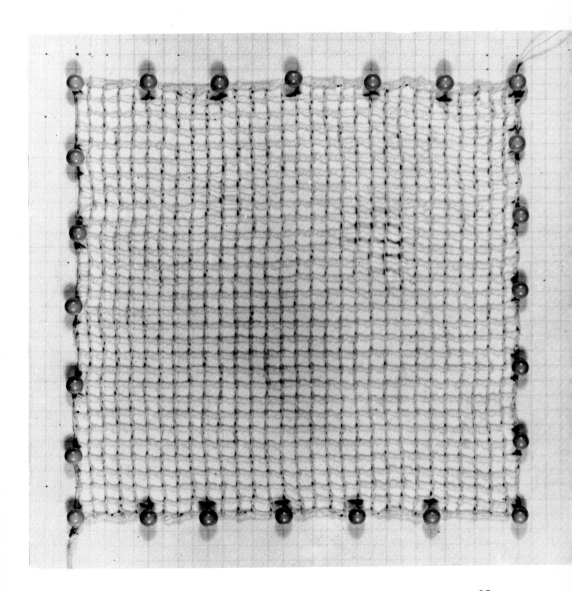

Diamond mesh net is stretched in the same way as the square mesh net in the preceding illustration. Notice the way the pins are placed in the outside meshes.

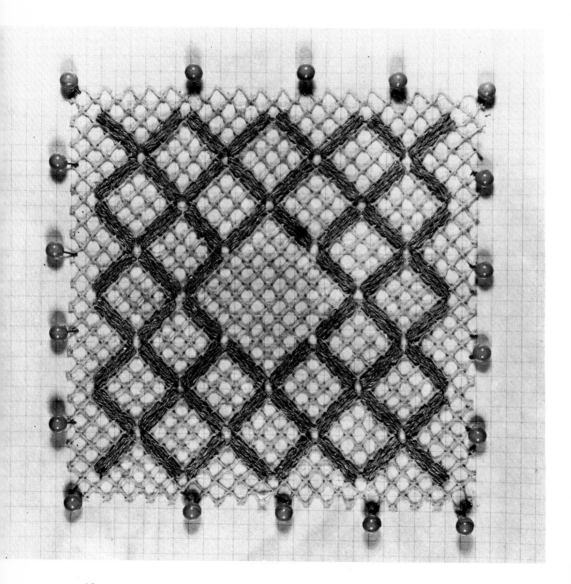

Here the net is stretched in a frame. The outside meshes are carefully pulled out and stretched with rug warp 12/6 or strong twine. Thread this into every or every other mesh and hook the cord round the nails on the outside of the frame.

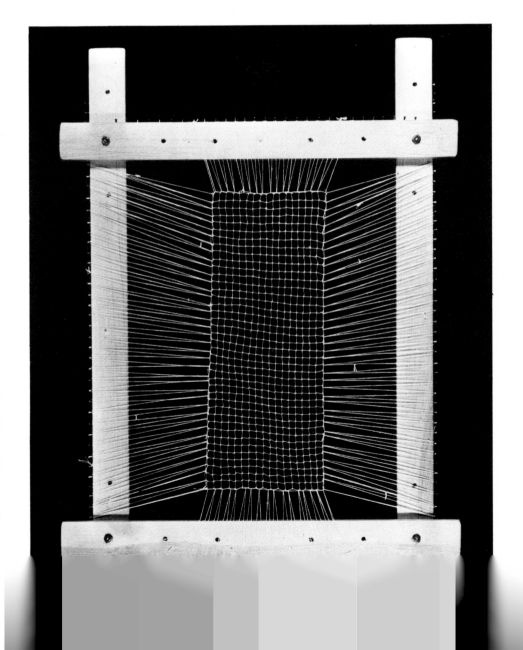

Embroidering patterns

For embroidering patterns the net should be mounted on a square or rectangular frame. On square mesh net use either the same kind of thread as was used for making the net or else a loosely-twisted linen yarn, for example Bocken's lace thread 18/3 or 18/5, depending on the size of the mesh. *Coton à broder,* stranded cotton and similar threads are also suitable. Use a blunt tapestry needle, size 18.

For embroidering patterns on diamond mesh net suitable threads are Holma Halsingland's linen yarn no. 16, half-bleached or unbleached, or NIAB's peasant thread, shades no. 603 and 604 (two attractive shades of pink) or no. 606 and 607 (blue). If you are not sure about the choice of colour white and unbleached linen yarn are always effective. The threads may be used single or double according to the size of the mesh.

The stitches most commonly used for embroidering on square mesh are the darning stitch (*point de reprise*) (see p. 43), the cloth (linen) stitch or *point de toile* (see p. 46), wheels (see p. 46) and the loop stitch (*point d'esprit*) (see pp. 44 and 45). Patterns embroidered on diamond mesh are usually worked in darning stitch and cross stitch (see p. 47).

 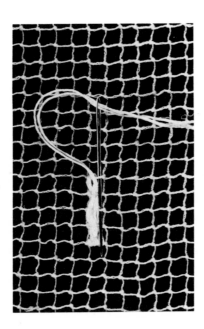 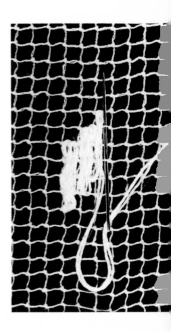

Double thread is sometimes used for darning stitch (*point de reprise*). Attach the thread by running the needle through the loop at the end (illustration on left).

For darning stitch, work backwards and forwards in a row of meshes until the holes are filled (centre illustration).

The illustration on the right shows how darning stitch is worked when the pattern slopes gradually upwards.

The filling stitch, known as the loop stitch or *point d'esprit,* which looks like open buttonhole stitch, is worked in rows backwards and forwards (see illustration). The thread is attached round one thread of a mesh, after which a loose loop is set in each mesh. The thread passes over the vertical and the following horizontal thread of the netting. The needle is always brought down from above under the netting thread and over the working thread (the thread you are sewing with). The loops should be large enough to cover half the mesh.

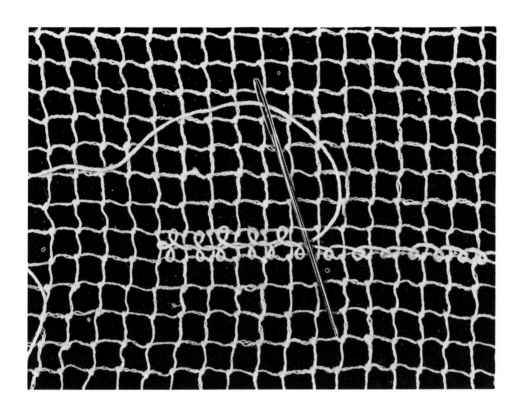

This illustration shows the completion of the *point d'esprit*. You work
the long buttonhole stitch as before but now carry each stitch round
the loop in the preceding row.

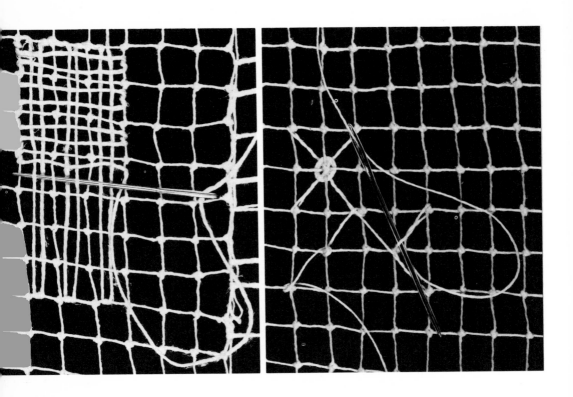

Cloth stitch (*point de toile*) is worked in two directions, the same way as for darning a hole (illustration on left). One or more meshes may be darned over, depending on the pattern, but the threads must cross each other regularly. Small extra stitches, to carry the thread over a thread in the net, are sometimes necessary in order to join up different figures in the pattern or to reach a part of the pattern that has not been previously worked.

Right-hand illustration. To make a wheel, as shown in the pattern on p. 68, run a thread from corner to corner of the mesh and then darn round, over and under the crossed threads.

Cross stitch worked on diamond mesh.

Making up

When the work is completed, remove it from the board or frame and lay it face downwards on some soft surface. Lay a piece of tissue paper on top and spray it all over with water. Pass a warm (not hot) iron over it. The work will then recover its stiff, fresh appearance.

If the net proves to be too large in relation to the embroidered pattern the meshes can be cut close to the knots, which will never come undone.

To make up cushions upon which to mount your netting, use only best quality down for the stuffing. Make a cover of thin linen and put the linen cushion into this. Then cut a piece of linen the same size as the netting and overcast three sides together from the wrong side. Turn the cover inside out, work the corners out with the fingers and then sew the fourth side together invisibly. A cord sewn round the edge makes a good finish. This should be made of several strands of linen thread 35/3.

To make up bags and purses on a frame cut the lining the same size as the netting and sew the two together with small stitches. Then sew up the sides of the bag and stitch it firmly to the inside of the frame. It is difficult to keep these stitches invisible and they are best covered with a cord made of a few linen threads.

'Envelope' bags should be stiffened with flannel or a double layer of Pelon (Vilene). It is easiest then to make up the lining and stiffening as a separate bag and insert this into the outer bag, which has already been completed.

Spectacle cases are made up on a framework of cardboard or canvas (hard, stiff lining material) of which two pieces are cut in the shape desired for the case. Then cut out four pieces of linen (allowing for a fastener at the seam) and sew them over the framework pieces. Sew the piece of netting on to one of the sides. Here again, a cord sewn round the case makes a suitable finish.

Lampshades may be made up on either a lining material or parchment. For square lampshades linen is the most suitable lining and has the right degree of translucency. For round lampshades parchment is easier to handle and looks better. For both square and round shades cover all the wires with 10 mm ($\frac{1}{2}$ in) strips of tricot or bias tape carefully stitched on. For square lampshades sew the lining material to the netting and sew the ends together from the wrong side. Turn the work and draw it over the frame, which it should fit quite tightly. Then stitch the material to the top and bottom edge of the frame.

For round shades cut the parchment 2 cm ($\frac{3}{4}$ in) longer than the circumference of the shade, lay the parchment all round and glue the edges or fasten them with sellotape. The parchment can if desired be covered with linen scrim. The ends of the netting are joined from the wrong side, the work turned inside out and drawn over the parchment. Finally, the work is stitched to the top and bottom edge of the frame.

In square mesh net the meshes along the edge come out double because of the increasing on both sides. To hide this and produce a straight edge a row of close buttonholing or double crochet may be worked along the edge, using the same thickness of thread as was used to make the net (see illustrations on p. 51).

If the finished work is used as an edging on a mat, sheet or pillow-case, sew it on with close buttonhole stitch using lace thread no. 60.

The illustration shows how the meshes may be cut close to the knot. This is often necessary with diamond mesh net, and there is no danger of the knots coming undone.

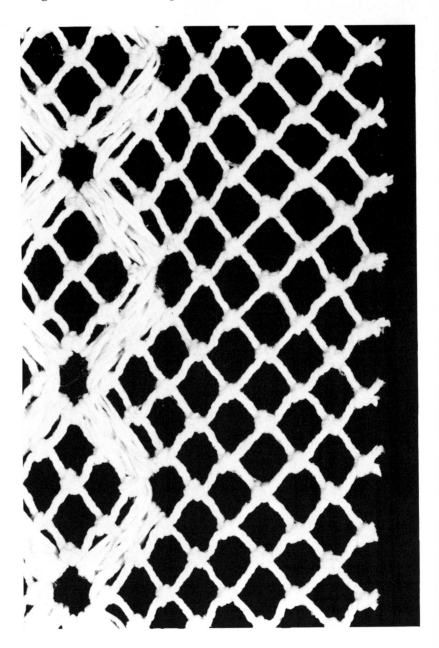

Close buttonhole stitch may be worked as a finish to the completed work. Use the same thread as for the net.

An edging of double crochet may also be used as a finish. Here again, use the same thread as for the net.

Detail of twisted and woven fringe

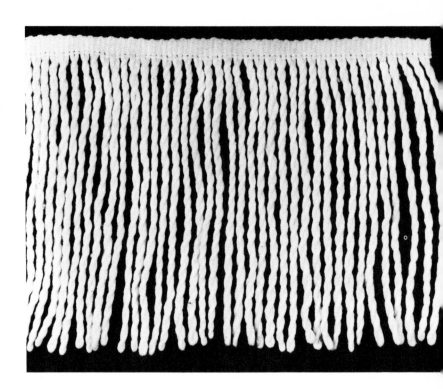

Cloths made at the beginning of the twentieth century are often finished with a fringe. This is made in a particular way in a belt loom. First make a warp of 10–15 threads of cotton yarn and thread it into the heddles. A coarse thread, usually rug warp, is heddled a little distance away, at the width you wish the fringe to be. The weft, which is used double, is wound on to a spool or bobbin and twisted together. This is passed first through one set of threads in the warp, then over and round the single thread and back through the other set of warp threads. The thread must be twisted tightly all the time. When the work reaches the required length, remove the single thread and you will have an even, close fringe.

The fringe twisted and woven on the loom as described on the previous page.

Original designs

If you want to design your own patterns, choose pattern shapes that are easy to translate into the particular technique of netting. The geometrical shapes that are easiest to work with are the square, the rectangle and the triangle. Use a piece of white paper as basis and draw in the outline of the work. Then cut out a number of pattern shapes in coloured paper and arrange them on the white paper in a design which, after experimenting, you find most suitable. The pattern must then be transferred to squared paper, for which 5 mm ($\frac{1}{4}$ in) paper is generally used. Draw in the pattern in the same way as for cross stitch, with lines or by filling in the squares. See illustrations on the opposite page.

Patterns that involve an even number of meshes always have a knot as the centre and patterns that cover an odd number of meshes always have a mesh as the centre.

On the left, a pattern in the cut-out stage; in the centre, a pattern transferred to squared paper; and right, the pattern worked on net.

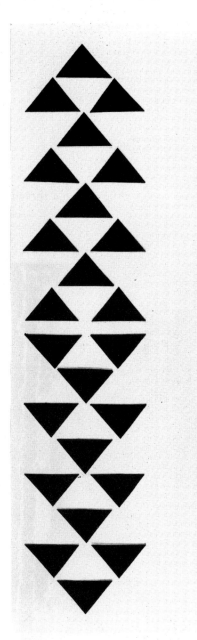
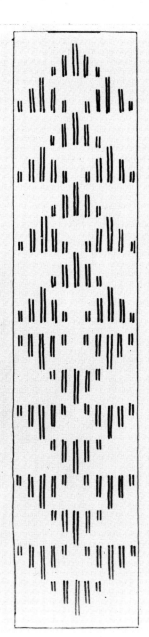
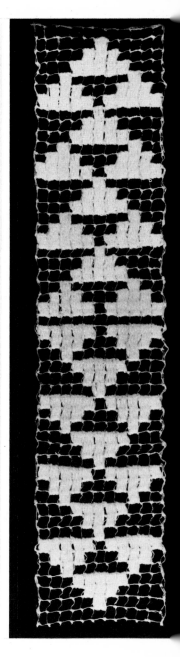

Examples

Pattern: Marita Persson
Size: 15 × 15 cm (6 × 6 in)
Net: 29 × 29 meshes with 5 mm ($\frac{1}{4}$ in) mesh stick and linen thread 35/3
Stitches: darning stitch in lace thread 18/5

Pattern: Alice Andersson
Size: 17·5 × 17·5 cm (6$\frac{7}{8}$ × 6$\frac{7}{8}$ in)
Net: 41 × 41 meshes with 4 mm ($\frac{3}{16}$ in) mesh stick and linen thread
35/3
Stitches: darning stitch in lace thread 18/5

Pattern: Ester Claesson
Size: 45 × 45 cm (18 × 18 in)
Net: 87 × 87 meshes with 5 mm ($\frac{1}{4}$ in) mesh stick and linen thread 35/3
Stitches: darning stitch in lace thread 18/5
Description of fringe on pp. 52 and 53.

Detail of cloth on previous page

Pattern: Ester Claesson
Size: 55 × 55 cm (22 × 22 in)
Net: 107 × 107 meshes with 5 mm ($\frac{1}{4}$ in) mesh stick and linen thread 35/3
Stitches: darning stitch in lace thread 18/5

Detail of cloth on previous page.

Size: 25 × 25 cm (10 × 10 in)
Net: 63 × 63 meshes with 4 mm ($\frac{3}{16}$ in) mesh stick and linen thread 35/3
Stitches: cloth stitch in linen thread 35/3 and outlining in lace thread 18/3. Crocheted edge in single crochet

Detail of pattern on previous page.

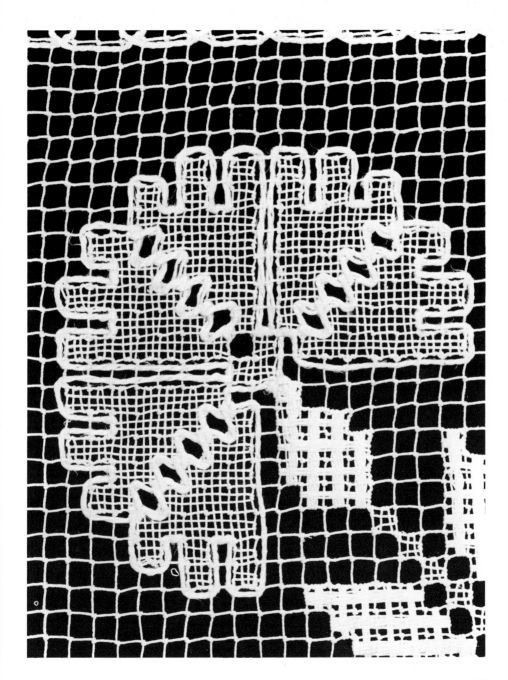

Size: 25 × 25 cm (10 × 10 in)
Net: 63 × 63 meshes with 4 mm ($\frac{3}{16}$ in) mesh stick and linen thread 35/3
Stitches: cloth stitch in linen thread 35/3 and outlining in lace thread 18/3. Crocheted edge in double crochet

Detail of pattern on previous page.

Pattern: Alice Andersson
Size: 17·5 × 17·5 cm ($6\frac{7}{8}$ × $6\frac{7}{8}$ in)
Net: 41 × 41 meshes with 4 mm ($\frac{3}{16}$ in) mesh stick and linen thread 35/3
Stitches: darning stitch in lace thread 18/5

Cushion

Size: 27 × 27 cm ($10\frac{3}{4}$ × $10\frac{3}{4}$ in)

Net: 70 × 70 meshes with 4 mm ($\frac{3}{16}$ in) mesh stick and linen thread 35/3

Stitches: darning stitch in linen thread 16/2

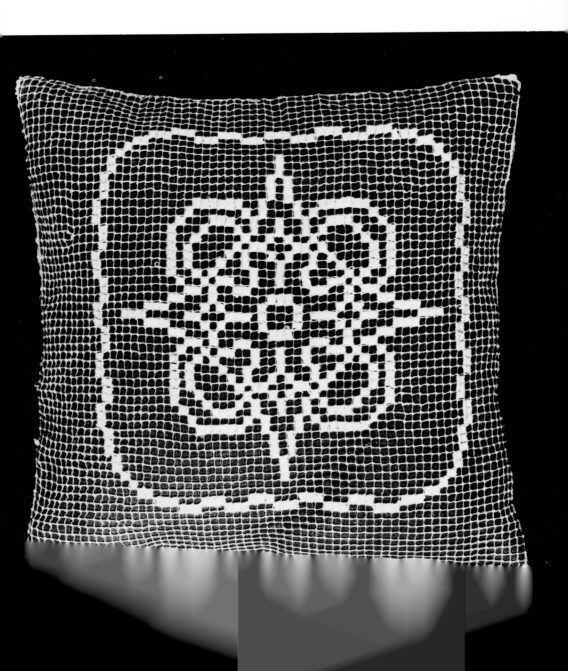

Lampshade in square mesh net. Copy of old pattern
Size: 14 × 30 cm (5½ × 12 in)
Net: 14 × 30 meshes with 10 mm (½ in) mesh stick and linen thread
35/3

Spectacle case
Size: 8 × 16 cm (3¼ × 6⅜ in)
Net: 39 × 39 meshes with 4 mm ($\frac{3}{16}$ in) mesh stick and linen thread 35/3
Stitches: darning stitch in linen thread 16/2

Pattern: Alice Andersson
Size: 13 × 13 cm (5¼ × 5¼ in)
Net: 26 × 26 meshes with 5 mm (¼ in) mesh stick and linen thread 35/5
Stitches: cloth stitch, whirls and *point d'esprit* in linen thread 35/3

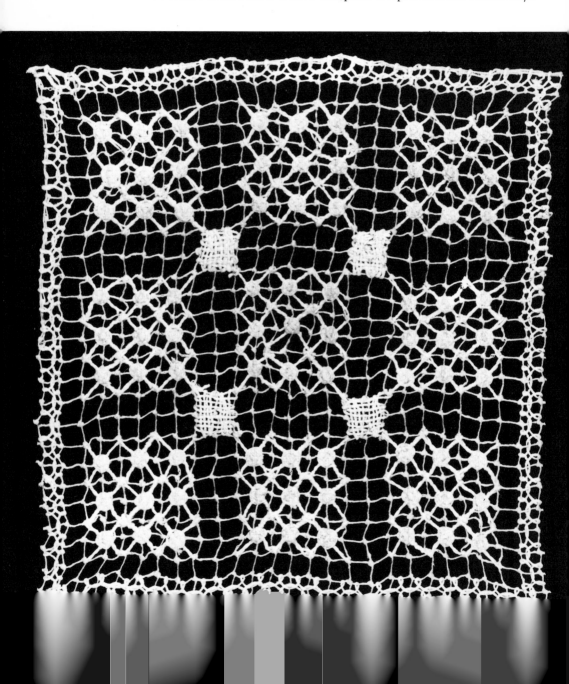

Pattern: Marita Persson
Size: 14 × 14 cm (5½ × 5½ in)
Net: 18 × 18 meshes with 5 mm (¼ in) mesh stick and linen thread 35/3
Stitches: darning stitch in linen thread 28/2, unbleached

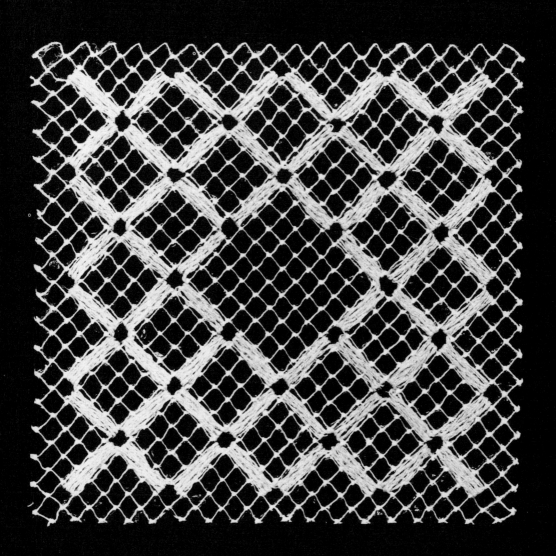

Mat in diamond mesh. Pattern from Hälsingeslöjd, Hudiksvall

Size: 18 × 18 cm (7¼ × 7¼ in)

Net: 29 × 29 meshes with 4 mm ($\frac{3}{16}$ in) mesh stick and linen thread 35/3

Stitches: darning stitch and cross stitch in NIAB's peasant yarn, colours no. 603 and 604

Pattern: Rut Pettersson
Size: about 58 cm (23 in) in diameter
Net: 4 mm ($\frac{3}{16}$ in) mesh stick; linen thread, unbleached and half-
bleached

Pattern: Lisa Melen
Size: 58 cm (23 in) in diameter
Net: mesh sticks of 5 ($\frac{1}{4}$ in) and 10 mm ($\frac{1}{2}$ in); linen thread 35/3, un-
bleached and half-bleached

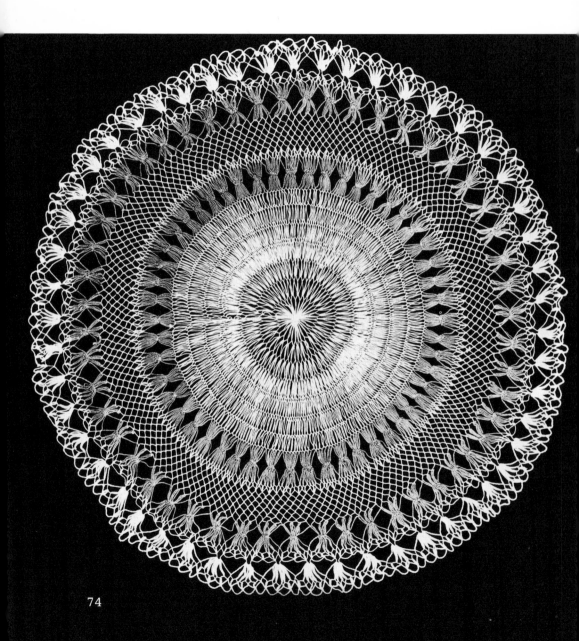

Patterns

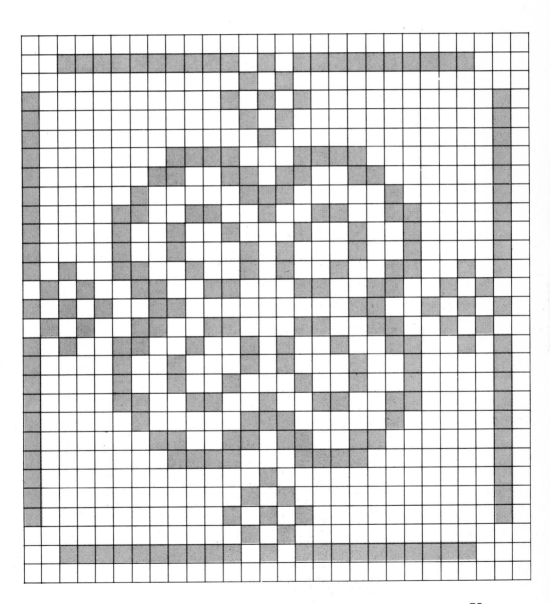

76

77

78

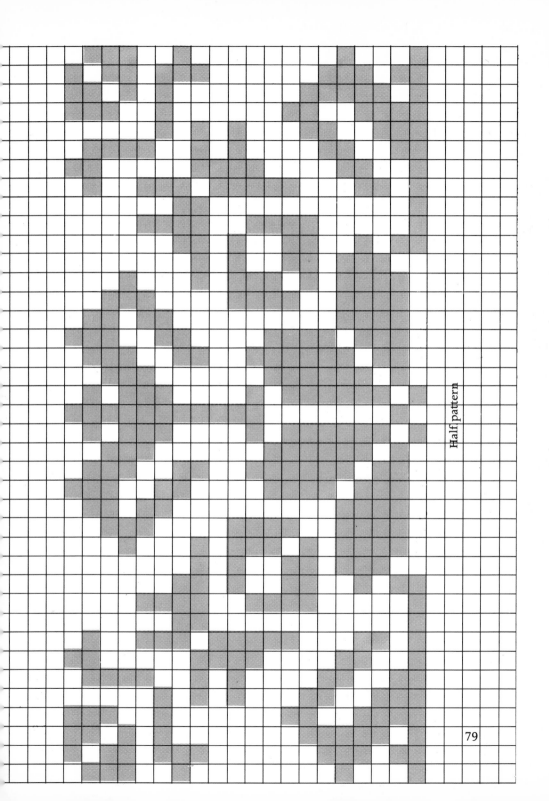

Half pattern

79

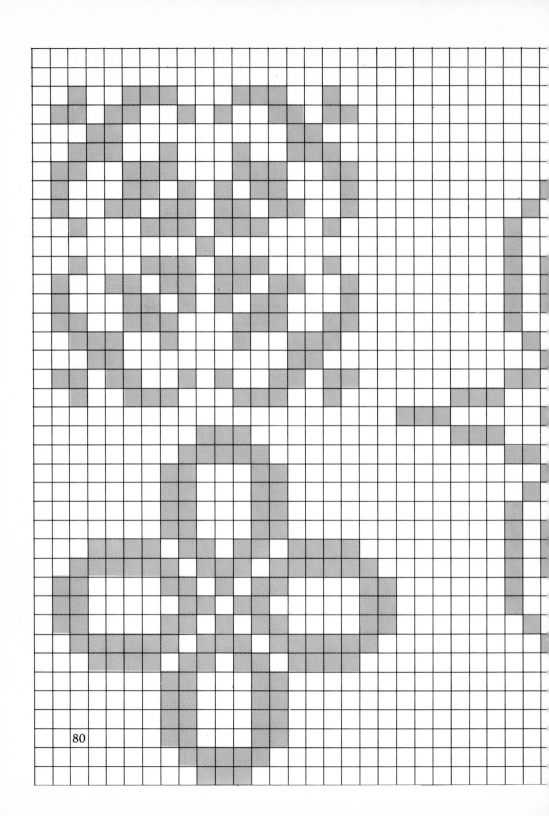

80

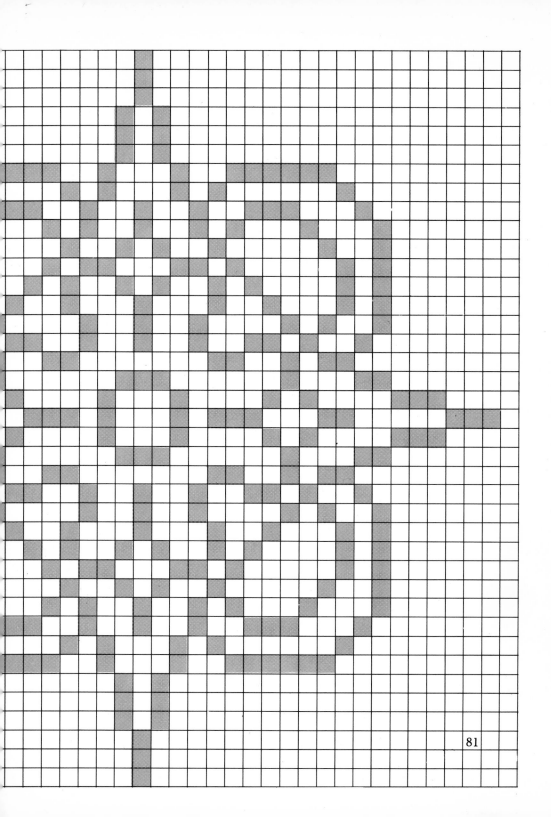

81

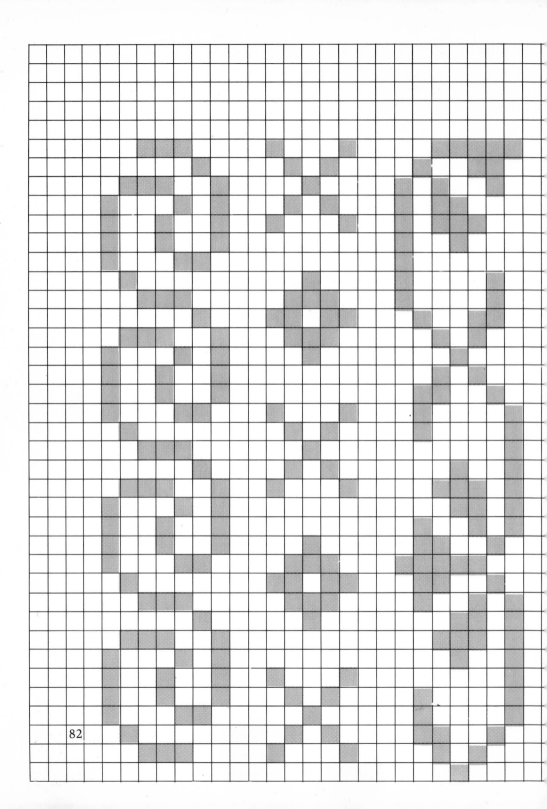

82

83

Half pattern

84

Half pattern

Half pattern

86

Half pattern

87